HE SPOKE TO HIMSELF

THAT MAKES YOU HIS OWN

EMMANUELA LEWIS

Published by Spines
ISBN: 979-8-89383-510-6

This book is dedicated to all the Evangelists, Pastors, Apostle, Prophet, Teachers, and Preachers who are daily proclaiming the good news to the world since it is the will of God following the footsteps of our Lord who also said He does nothing of Himself but only what He has seen His father do, for blessed and beautiful are the feet of those who bring good news and proclaim peace, good tidings and salvation to the people saying to Zion or to people your God reigns. May the Good Lord be glorified repeatedly every day through them in the name of our Lord Jesus Christ Amen

CONTENTS

GREETINGS

Greetings to you in the name of our Lord God.

I hope I have found you well as we are all journaling through this Life and its many issues, but with all that is going on if you are among the living then I thank God for your life because this is a sign of victory. For some made a choice not to continue with this war called LIFE and has given up HOPE on all fronts, and without hope, there is nothing to live for, so may grace and peace be multiplied to you and most importantly blessed be the God of our Lord who according to His abundant mercy has made it possible for you and your love once to behold today. We thank Him for His goodness in your lives and may He be glorified in everything you do, may He bless you as you are going out and your coming in and keep you in our Lord Jesus Name. Amen.

INTRODUCTION

If you are wondering why l am in your hands or why l am in your home through this book, well what can l say other than to tell you that you and l have been given another chance to make things right again as living beings and as God's handy work? Every day we wake from our sleep, which is a calm journey knowing where our destination is going to be and that is to awake but it does not happen to many. It is just by the Grace of God that you and I get the chance to see another day for it has nothing to do with the sound of our alarms. We can place an ALARM beside a dead person and see if they can be awake by it not to talk about the various ways that take the life of others, and so the Lord God expects us to live a better life than we did yesterday., l am here through this book to tell you that God wants to be more involved in your life to help you through it all since He created it you and this world.

My name is Emmanuela Lewis, and you can call me Miss Peggy. I am an Author and an Evangelist of our Lord God who has directed me to bring you incredibly GOOD NEWS through this book, that His mercy is and has been calling you from behind every day including today through this book which is a letter from Him to you. So that is why I have come to your home and my prayer is may you respond to this letter from your marker.

FOREWORD

You might not be having a good day, or you are having a good day, but things are going to change right now as you read this good news

And before we get to it, let me make you laugh a little by telling you a joke.

There was a man who always said to his wife I love you and I will die for you, and so one day he noticed that his wife's countenance had changed and he said to the wife why has your countenance changed what is the problem, why is your face sad since you are not sick, this is nothing but sorrow of the heart. I think you know that I love you and I will die for you right? And the wife answered by saying to him, you kept telling me you love me, and you will die for me, but you have not proven it to me by killing yourself.

YOU WERE HIS BEFORE YOU WERE NOT

Then they asked Him, saying, "Teacher, we know that You say and teach rightly, and You do not show personal favoritism, but teach the way of God in truth."

"Is it lawful for us to pay taxes to Caesar or not?"

But He perceived their craftiness, and said to them, "Why do you test Me?" Show Me a denarius. Whose image and inscription does it have?" They answered and said, "Caesar's."

And He said to them, "Render therefore to Caesar the things that are Caesar's, and to God the things that are God's."

— LUKE 20:21-25

The Lord asked them to show Him the image of that country's currency, which is called the denarius and when they did, He asked them whose image and inscription does it have? "And they answered and said, "Caesar's." "So, He said to them, "Render therefore to Caesar the things that are Caesar's, and to God the things that are God's." The understanding I want you to get from this scripture is that HUMANITY was created in the image of God, He created us in His own image

So, we belong to Him and to Him alone. Let us see how we were created

> Then God said, "Let the waters abound with an abundance of living creatures, and let birds fly above the earth across the face of the firmament of the heavens."
>
> Then God said, "Let the earth bring forth the living creature according to its kind: cattle and creeping things and beasts of the earth, each according to its kind"; and it was so.
>
> — GENESIS 1:20-24

> Then God said, "Let the earth bring forth grass, the herb that yields seed, and the fruit tree that yields fruit according to its kind, whose seed is in itself, on the earth"; and it was so.
>
> — GENESIS 1:11

When God was creating the world, He spoke to the waters to abound with an abundance of living creatures, and it was so. He spoke to the Earth, "Let the Earth bring forth the living creature according to its kind: cattle and creeping things and beasts of the Earth, each according to its kind"; and it was so. Let the earth bring forth grass, the herb that yields seed, and the fruit tree that yields fruit according to its kind, whose seed is in itself, on the earth;" and it was so. And none of this can survive without its source. Let the earth bring forth grass. If you uproot a tree from the ground the end of it is death because it is disconnected from its source. Let the waters abound with an abundance of living creatures. If you disconnect a fish from the water the end of it is nothing but death.

Then God said, "Let Us make man in Our image, according to Our likeness;

— GENESIS 1:26A

And the Lord God formed man of the dust of the ground, and breathed into his nostrils the breath of life, and man became a living being.

— GENESIS 2:7

When God got to the turn of creating men, He did not speak to the earth nor the waters, but HE SPOKE TO HIMSELF by saying Let Us make men in Our image, according to Our likeness; so, men are the source of God Himself. How then can we live and function well if we are not connected to our source? Before He formed you in the womb of your mother even though your parents knew you not and cannot even describe you because you were still in the womb, your God who put you in there knew you and everything about you before you were even born. That's why He alone is your help in this land of the living just as you cannot take a broken car to a doctor to fix it, nor take a wound to a mechanic to treat. When we look around us it's true that God by His grace has given men wisdom to invent things and when there is a problem with it, the manufacturers or those who are knowledgeable are the ones to fix them. That is why no man nor anything in this world can give your lost and broken soul rest but the God who created you, I know you can attest that nothing in this world can give your soul rest be it men, wealth, substance, alcohol and whatever is found out there., Ask God for help for He is waiting for you, you were His before you were not, we were ditched from Him because of the fall of men through our parents Adam and Eve thanks to the Devil who made himself our adversary just to see us fail but God's mercy said NO by Him coming to redeem us.

THE REASON WHY JESUS IS LORD

For there are three that bear witness in heaven: the
Father, the Word, and the Holy Spirit; and these three
are one.

— 1 JOHN 5:7

God is one but magnifies Himself in three offices. Just as He
spoke to Himself and brought us forth, He also spoke to His
Word and turned it into a person called Jesus Christ and His
breath into another person called the Holy Spirit and these
three are one. So, when you say scripture or bible what you
mean is Jesus Christ for, He is the Word of God and so when
someone says 1 believe in God but 1 does not believe in Jesus
Christ what they are saying is God has never spoken. But Jesus
is Lord because God spoke everything into existence by saying
Let there be this and let there be that and it was so, to separate
Christ from God is like you being separated from your own
words or your voice which is not possible.

In the beginning was the Word, and the Word was with God, and the Word was God. He was in the beginning with God. All things were made through Him, and without Him, nothing was made that was made. In Him was life, and the life was the light of men.

— JOHN 1:1-4

For by Him all things were created that are in heaven and that are on earth, visible and invisible, whether thrones or dominions or principalities or powers. All things were created through Him and for Him. And He is before all things, and in Him all things consist.

— COLOSSIANS 1:16-17

Jesus is not just someone claiming to be God. He is indeed the IAM This is why Jesus Christ has to be the center of your life if you acknowledge the existence of God then you should acknowledge the existence of the voice or the Word of God too, all things were created through Him and for Him, all things consist in Him without Him nothing was made that was made for God created this world by speaking.

"Let not your heart be troubled; you believe in God, believe also in Me.

— JOHN 14: 1

Without Christ in your life, it's like grabbing something without your tomb and we know how that will go, that is why we do not have the true joy we are looking for in whatever money can buy and from people, etc. His life is the light of men So you will not find REST anywhere to fill that vacuum you have within you, but only in Him for in Him is where God placed life which is the light of men, salvation cannot come from anywhere but through Jesus the Christ.

WEALTH IS JUST A TOOL AND NOTHING MORE

Because you say, 'I am rich, have become wealthy, and need nothing'—and do not know that you are wretched, miserable, poor, blind, and naked—

— REVELATION 3:17

You will attest with me that we do not refer to someone who is rich and wealthy as wretched, miserable, poor, blind, and naked, but God is saying for someone to say I am rich, I have become wealthy and in need of nothing because of wealth — this person is standing on sinking sand and it's just a matter of time before the unexpected happens. for the truth is wealth is just a tool and nothing else.

You can buy a golden bed and sleep on it because you can afford it, but that golden bed cannot promise you good sleep nor promise you the next day.

You can have all the organic food in your fridge but it cannot promise you an appetite.

You can marry whoever you want but you are not promised a peaceful home.

You can buy whatever car you want but it cannot promise you a safe journey.

You can build whatever mansion you want and put all the experienced security men and all the expensive cameras in there but you are not guaranteed loyal people, there is a saying in my country that says those you eat with are the ones who will consume your meat, you know your enemies and can do your best to protect yourself from them but those you eat and laugh with are the most dangerous people around you, no one has ever said his or her enemy has broken their trust, it's our love once who can break our trust. That's how crafty the enemy who has made himself our adversary is, There is no true satisfaction for us in anything, for they are just tools to help us live life , and so if that is what you have placed your hope and your joy in, then you can understand why God is saying you are the most wretched, miserable, poor, blind, and naked person, He is the only one who is your anchor in this land of the living and wealth cannot even redeem your soul.

"Ho! Everyone who thirsts, Come to the waters; And you who have no money, Come, buy and eat. Yes, come, buy wine and milk Without money and without price. Why do you spend money for what is not bread, And your wages for what does not satisfy? Listen carefully to Me, and eat what is good, And let your soul delight itself in abundance. Incline your ear, and come to Me.

— ISAIAH 55:1-3

Hear, and your soul shall live; And I will make an everlasting covenant with you—The sure mercies of David.

God created everything in this world including all the wealth and so if these things were enough to redeem us we know that He would not have had a problem at all, but wealth was not enough to purchase your soul is why He is saying do not spend money on what is not bread, for everything money can buy is not the true BREAD to satisfy the soul you cannot give your soul rest by yourself He had to come down Himself because He has to pay with His blood that is how expensive you are, the whole wealth in this world was not enough to redeem your soul you cost Him His Blood. and this is the goodness of God even though it cast Him His life as freedom is not free yet He is calling everyone to Come to the salvation waters; and buy without a price because He has paid it in full on our behalf, invitation is given to special people or those we care about and He has given you an invitation to the Abundant Life He alone can offer, that is how special you are to Him, ask your fingerprint if there are two like you there are no two like you and if you are the only one living on this planet He would have still gone through this pain to redeem you. You are invited please accept the invitation.

GOD'S PLAN TO SAVE MANKIND IN HIS TIMING

All who dwell on the earth will worship him, whose names have not been written in the Book of Life of the Lamb slain from the foundation of the world.

— REVELATION 13:8

God is omnipotent He knew before the foundation of the world that one of His creations called Lucifer would later cause our downfall. And made provisions by slaying our Lord before He ever said let there be this and let there be that, for He sacrificed our Lord Jesus Christ before He Laid the foundation of this world. but His name Jesus Christ was not written in the Book of Life in those days, God whose wisdom is past finding out decided to hide His name Jesus Christ from our fathers. but something amazing happened, our fathers never knew that as they were naming their children God was busy speaking Mistry to them through the names they were given their children, and in those days names were given based on the situation that was going on before and throughout the pregnancy.

We could pick up the intention of God through those names given, these names and their meanings tell us that when God said the thoughts, He has towards us are not evil but to give us hope and a future is indeed the TRUTH. All His thoughts towards us are to save us back to Himself and as they were naming their children God's agenda was all over them, this is the question King Solomon asks in the book of Proverbs, can a man's ways be found in him or herself and the answer is certainty not, the earth is the Lords and the fullness there off indeed. These are the meanings of these names:

God
Adam = Man / Genesis 1:27
Seth = Appointed / Genesis 4:25
Enosh = mortal / Genesis 4:26
Cainan = sorrow / Genesis 5:9
Mahalalel = the blessed God / Genesis 5:12
Jared = Shall come down / Genesis 5:15
Enoch = Teaching / Genesis 5:18
Methuselah = His death shall bring / Genesis 5:21
Lamech = the despairing / Genesis 5:25
Noah = Comfort or Rest. /Genesis 5:28-29

Putting them together is Man is appointed, a mortal man of sorrow is born, the blessed God shall come down and teach that His death shall bring the grieving or the despairing comfort and rest

But the Lord is faithful, who will establish you and guard you from the evil one.

— 2 THESSALONIANS 3:3

He who has promised you is faithful and has been faithful when the time came for Him to do what He says He will do He come through for us, there is nothing He has promised you that He will not do because He cannot deny Himself that He is faithful in all His ways.

> Forever, O Lord, Your word is settled in heaven. Your faithfulness endures to all generations; You established the earth, and it abides.
>
> — PSALMS 119:89-90

Just as He has established the earth and made it abide because He told the earth to abide He said His thoughts towards you are to give you an expected end and even though the enemy also has his thoughts towards you that he will do everything in his power for you not to come to the faith of our Lord Jesus Christ God Word is what is settled in heaven, any other words will pass away for His steadfast love for you has not and will never ceased, Him dyeing for you should tell you that.

GOD HID THIS MYSTERY FROM OUR FATHER'S

The mystery which has been hidden from ages and from generations, but now has been revealed to His saints. To them God willed to make known what the riches of the glory of this mystery among the Gentiles are: which is Christ in you, the hope of glory.

— COLOSSIANS 1:26-27

God decided to hide this mystery from our fathers that He has made provisions to redeem us and will descend through His Word Jesus Christ who will come down at an appointed time to save not only the Jews but we the Gentiles too from all our sins through His death on the cross, but now it has been revealed to His saints which is our generation according to His good pleasure which He purposed in Himself, God willed to make known what the riches of the glory of this mystery among the Gentiles are: among anyone who has come to know the faith and all those who are on their way coming to the faith that CHRIST IN US IS THE HOPE OF GLORY that we the

Gentiles save by grace can also cry out to Him Abba Father for we have become heirs together with Christ in one kingdom we have been given the power to become children of God.

And she will bring forth a Son, and you shall call His name Jesus, for He will save His people from their sins."

— MATTHEW 1:21

And the Word became flesh and dwelt among us, and we beheld His glory, the glory as of the only begotten of the Father, full of grace and truth.

— JOHN 1:14

God's Word and promise became flesh in the name of our Lord Jesus who dwelt among us and accomplished the purpose for which He came down which is to die for our sins so that we can become His righteousness in Him which means we are no longer course but bless in Him for we have been acquitted and justified, that's the manner of love the Father has bestowed on you.

Blessed be the God and Father of our Lord Jesus Christ, who has blessed us with every spiritual blessing in the heavenly places in Christ,

— EPHESIANS 1:3

having made known to us the mystery of His will, according to His good pleasure which He purposed in Himself, that in the dispensation of the fullness of the times He might gather together in one all things in

Christ, both which are in heaven, and which are on earth—in Him.

— EPHESIANS 1:9-10

God has shown and proven that He cares for our souls not just in words but with deeds by delivering us from internal destruction which we rightfully deserve so that in the dispensation of the fullness of the times He might gather together in one all things in Christ, both which are in heaven, and which are on earth—in Him. it is your turn to also come and wash in the blood, what l want to tell you is that He is truly Lord and can you imagine this Almighty God leaving His thrown to come down and go through that pain just for your sake, He has done everything He has to do prove to you that He is the only person who cares about you, and you may say your sins are great His love and His mercies are much more abounds and there is no sin His blood cannot cleans so come as you, we all came just as we were, we did not have any good deeds to bring to the salvation table if we do He wouldn't have come for our rescue, Salvation is a gift to receive not a goal to achieve for anyone to boasts about, all have sinned and short of His glory, but because of Christ righteousness we can now behold His Glory.

YOUR FATHER IS LOOKING
FOR YOU

And Jesus said to him, "Today salvation has come to this house, because he also is a son of Abraham; for the Son of Man has come to seek and to save that which was lost."

— LUKE 19:9-10

There is a difference between someone who must save another from whatever situation they are in because they happened to be around, and someone who is intentionally seeking people who need to be saved, the job of our Lord Jesus is seeking the lost sons and daughters who are the descendants of Abraham and those who have become the descendants of Abraham through adoption which is open to all who are not Jews like you and me, Jesus came to save sinners of all classes, genders, and ethnicities, young and old, powerful and the forgotten EVERYONE who will be admitted that they are lost and in need of a saviour, for to be able to save someone they would have to admit that they are lost.

But it is not that the word of God has taken no effect. For they are not all Israel who are of Israel, nor are they all children because they are the seed of Abraham; but, "In Isaac your seed shall be called."

— ROMANS 9:6-7

Some rejection of the gospel of our Lord Jesus's Purpose to save their souls is not that the Word of God has taken no effect. The reason for the rejection from some is because not all Israel who are of Israel nor are they all children because they are the seed of Abraham; but "In Isaac, seed shall be called." The scripture is saying even though Christ died for the whole world as the Word says because of Gods love for the world He gave His only begotten son that WHOSOEVER believes in Him will be saved, that has been already established meaning God has done His part but our response to the call is an indication as to why some of us have hidden our heart concerning the salvation of our soul, but what we know is, our Lord said He has an assignment to fulfil and that assignment is to bring mankind who are the image of God back to God and none of those given to Him will remain missing. God will bring them home through WHATEVER means and give their soul rest and knowing that they have a place in the bosom of Abraham because it is a predestined movement situation gives those of us who have accepted the the gift of salvation a peace of mind, l have never heard a parent whose child got lost said l have more children here so we are not going to look or search for our missing child and if we motel man will go to whatever lent to look for that child till he or she is found, you can imagine what lent the good Lord will go for His lost children, For you to even here the call of God from me through this book is a very big testimony of its own, which should tell you that none of Gods children will remain missing INDEED, 1 was lost too and NOW am found to pass on the good news to others, God can use anyone to accomplish His plans and purposes so we are rest assured YOU will come to the faith for God has weaponised people, circumstances' and situation to draw your attention to SAVE you.

I say to you that likewise there will be more joy in heaven over one sinner who repents than over ninety-nine just persons who need no repentance.

— LUKE 15:7

The Lord your God in your midst,

— ZEPHANIAH 3:17

The Mighty One, will save; He will rejoice over you with glad-ness, He will quiet you with His love, He will rejoice over you with singing."

Likewise, I say to you, there is joy in the presence of the angels of God over one sinner who repents."

— LUKE 15:10

There is a party awaiting your repentance and Is not only us or the angels who rejoice for your homecoming but God Himself rejoices over you with gladness, He will quiet you with His love, and He will rejoice over you with singing." this is Amazing love indeed form the Almighty God who needs no one to complete Him because He is complete by Himself but looks at how important you are to the kingdom of God, this was David's Thanksgiving to God, David went to the temple of God and sat before the Lord; and he said: "Who am I, O Lord God? And what is my house, that You have brought me this far? and my personal question to our Lord God sometimes too is, if we say we serve the Lord, what does that mean, because we do not cook for Him nor wash His clothes He is the air we breathe, our protection, our shelter, our healer, our peace, our joy, our hope, the husband to the widow, the father to the fatherless, our help and our everything so then who is serving who it's not God doing all the serving thing? I know you can see clearly that no one will love and care for you like this God.

GOD'S LOVE FOR THE WORLD

For God so loved the world that He gave His only begotten Son, that whoever believes in Him should not perish but have everlasting life.

— JOHN 3:16

Do not love the world or the things in the world. If anyone loves the world, the love of the Father is not in him.

— JOHN 2:15

God loves the World but we are told not to love the World, Do you know why, the reason is this, The difference between God's love and men's love is that God's love for the world caused Him to GIVE us everything and most importantly even His life as He laid down His love for us on the cross so that we might live internally. but we love the world and demonstrate it by TAKING, according to our understanding of the fallen men-centred system which is our way of what we call life, loving the world to us means taking whatever we can get our hands on, our love for the world causes us to take from it and zero love for the one who created the world and the things in it, but God's love for the world causes Him to give everything to it, He is the gift that keeps giving this demonstrates His true love toward us, what you should know is that, no one will ever love you like Him, His love is called AGAPE LOVE which makes Him the only one to place your total life in because of His true thoughts towards you.

> What then shall we say to these things? If God is for us, who can be against us? He who did not spare His own Son, but delivered Him up for us all, how shall He not with Him also freely give us all things?

> — ROMANS 8:31-32

This is God's everlasting Love for you, what else would He not do for you after putting His son through all this on your behalf, He was rejected by His father on the cross, and is not because of ANYTHING He has done but because of EVERY-THING we have done. He said to His father why have you forsaken me, Nothing should stand between you and this loving God who is standing at the door of your heart knocking day and night, He can choose to come in by force but would that be seen as love? forcing someone to do something is not done out of love because it is not out of the will of that person, that is why even though He can make us serve Him, just like a dictator, instead He wants you to respond to His call my opening the door of your heart yourself, it should be because it is what you want to do, in this way, you can serve Him with love in response to His first love towards you, for He first love us we are just responding to His love for us and what then shall we say to these things? If God is for us, who can be against us? He who did not spare His own Son, but delivered Him up for us all, how shall He not with Him also freely give us all things? Christ is for all humanity, but would you receive Him today since tomorrow promises no one?

YOU CANNOT GOOD YOUR WAY IN

Help us, O God of our salvation, For the glory of Your name;

And deliver us, and provide atonement for our sins, For Your name's sake!

God indeed did provide atonement for our sins, For His name's sake, He investigated His love in which He loves us and sacrificed His beloved son for us not because we did anything to deserve it. He just cannot deny Himself that He is good, and His mercies endure forever. this conveys themes of repentance, restoration, and acknowledging God's sovereignty. As we all know, the only thing mankind is good at is sin which should rightfully lead us to destruction where we belong since we cannot sew pepper and expect to ripe tomato, but His mercy said No and rather paved the way for us to be redeemed from the hands of the enemy through the finished work of the cross.

> For by grace you have been saved through faith, and that not of yourselves; it is the gift of God, not of works, lest anyone should boast.

> — EPHESIANS 2:8-9

What this means is as l was saying, there is nothing men can do by our strength that will earn us a sport in the kingdom of God, it does not matter who did what and who did not do what no one can say my sins were on the lower or smaller shelves and not on the higher or bigger shelves like others, etc. or am not that sinner like others and that is why l got me salvation, just as men likes to categorise sin, if we indeed take pressure in what we think we can do then according to God if you broke one of His laws you have broken them all, that is the golden rule it has nothing to do with works, lest anyone should boast, so do not see yourself as somebody who is beyond salvation because of what you have done or because of the kind of life you have lived, it does not matter the blood of Jesus is still the remedy, there is no search thing like let me get my art together then l can come to Him, we can't get our act together because of our sinful nature, a tree has no option but to produce its kind and that is what we do, He has to do it that is Gods job, we come just as we are and after washing us, sanctified us, and justified us, there will be a time where we would not like to live the life we use to live anymore, for it will not bring us the joy anymore as it used to because of the power of God that has taken His dwelling in us after receiving the gift of salvation, having the nature of God is what enables us live a godly life.

Therefore if the Son makes you free, you shall be free indeed.

— JOHN 8:36

Having wiped out the handwriting of requirements that was against us, which was contrary to us. And He has taken it out of the way, having nailed it to the cross.

— COLOSSIANS 2:14

It used to be, get your art together before you come to me, before l bless you and so on, which was contrary to us because it was impossible for us not to sin looking at our nature, and so God through Christ wiped out all that handwriting containing the requirements that were against us having nailed it to the cross, just Come as you are and receive the gift of salvation for your soul is anxiously waiting for rest love yourself that much, your Faith in Christ is all it required to be save just as Abraham believe and was counted to him as righteousness and with the help of the holy spirit progressively change will happened that is what salvation does to us.

Whatever we choose to do with it, we will eat the fruits of it, what l want to tell you is this, as someone who has the nature of God you can proclaim the things you want to see tomorrow, not the situation. He is the way the truth and the life.

And where I go you know, and the way you know. Thomas said to Him, "Lord, we do not know where You are going, and how can we know the way?"

Jesus said to him, "I am the way, the truth, and the life. No one comes to the Father except through Me.

"If you had known Me, you would have known My Father also; and from now on you know Him and have seen Him."

— JOHN 14:5-7

In my country, Ghana, there is a word of knowledge our parent and the elderly says to us and it goes like this, SHOW ME YOUR FRIEND AND I WILL SHOW YOU YOUR CHARACTER anytime you hear this phrase from an Elderly what she or he means or what they are saying to you is you are not living a good life so WARCH OUT, for you are on the same path your friend is walking on, it just a matter of time for you to be just like her as you two continue to walk together. Birds with the same feathers flow together.

Thomas one of the disciples of our Lord Jesus Christ said to Him, "Lord, we do not know where You are going, and how can we know the way?" they want to know the WAY because When you are walking with someone and the person's life pleases you, you want to walk the same walk, as it's written that "Stand in the ways and see, and ask for the old paths, where the good way is, and walk in it; they knew going the same way is LIFE since this world is not intended to be a permanent place for us to dwell, and Jesus said to him, "I am the way, the truth, and the life. No one comes to the Father except through Me. All our Lord is saying to them and us is you do not need to look far personally the way to the place you want to go the only highway to Heaven, and if you do not know, from now on you know. the truth that sets you free.

For by Him all things were created that are in heaven and that are on earth, visible and invisible, whether thrones or dominions or principalities or powers. All things were created through Him and for Him. And He is before all things, and in Him all things consist. And He is the head of the body, the church, who is the beginning, the firstborn from the dead, that in all things He may have the preeminence.

— COLOSSIANS 1:16-18

Nor is there salvation in any other, for there is no other name under heaven given among men by which we must be saved."

— ACTS 4:12

Christ is the PREEMINENT in all things, the darkness of sin has engulfed us, and we need a saviour to set our soul free from internal destruction We need a saviour we will be able to call upon in this life and its many issues, and we know it's only God who can save us and God has made it clear that His WORD-JESUS is what He created this world with, is what should lead us to Him to be saved, because of our sins Christ is our Atonement so no one can go to the father except through Him. Salvation comes from the Lord God, there is no other name given to us to save but only in the name of Jesus.

Just as, if you need something and what you need is with certain people in a certain country who speak and understand only in their language what do you do, you have to Speak their language for them to understand you for you to get what you want This is what Almighty God is saying that He only speaks, does things and understands in His language and that language is JESUS CHRIST.

GOD DOES NOT HAVE GRANDCHILDREN

"I will be a Father to you, And you shall be My sons and daughters, Says the Lord Almighty."

— 2 CORINTHIANS 6:18

Sons and Heirs For you are all sons of God through faith in Christ Jesus.

— GALATIANS 3:26

Behold what manner of love the Father has bestowed on us, that we should be called children of God!

Beloved, now we are children of God.

— 1 JOHN 3:1A-2A

Salvation is a personal journey and so even if you were born into a church or your family took you to church throughout your childhood but you have not taken the personal decision to declare your faith in Him, it means you are not His child, we are not a Christians because we were born and grew up in church nor our family took us to church, without our proclaiming the Lordship of our Lord Jesus personally all we are is just church attendee as He said in Matthew 7:21:

"Not everyone who says to Me, 'Lord, Lord,' shall enter the kingdom of heaven, but he who does the will of My Father in heaven.

— MATTHEW 7:21

It's because they have not taken the decision to confess the Lordship of our Lord Jesus Christ to partake of the inheritance given to us through the finished work on the cross even though they are always in the house of God saying to Him Lord, Lord, but has not done the WILL of the father by going through the ADOPTION process, He does not have grandchildren only sons and daughters, He is looking forward to be a Father to you, and you shall be His sons and daughters so you can call Him Abba Father as His adopted child.

Who is he who overcomes the world, but he who believes that Jesus is the Son of God?

— 1 JOHN 5:5

The only people who have overcome the world are those who believe that Jesus is the Son of God since everything was created in Him and for Him, and He is the one who judges and rewards and instead of declaring us guilty He said not guilty all because we believe in who He says He is, He is "The one who courses the barren to have seven children, He kills and makes alive; He brings down to the grave and brings up. He raises the poor from the dust and lifts the beggars from the ash heap, to set them among princes and make them inherit the throne of glory. "For the pillars of the earth are the Lord's, and He has set the world upon them. Do you now understand why those who believe are overcomers? I believe that you are ready to partake in this Christ-like walk the next page will lead you to confess Christ as your Lord and your personal saviour and become one of the Over-comers all in the name of Jesus Christ.

SALVATION PRAYER REDEMPTION IN CHRIST

Blessed be the God and Father of our Lord Jesus Christ, who has blessed us with every spiritual blessing in the heavenly places in Christ,

— EPHESIANS 1:3

Receive this gift with meekness the implanted Word Jesus Christ, who is able to save your soul and the only chance to heavenly glorification, for those that believe He gave them the power to become His children as He overrules all of our failures and the self-blames because He offers us total forgiveness. You are holding this book because you are path to the redemption of the Lord or among those Jesus Christ died for, nothing just happened everything happened for a reason you did not just stumble on this TRUTH someone has been praying for you including me, even though Faith comes by hearing it does not end there, for whatever information you hear it all comes down to what you do with that information, you are about to act on what you have heard me say throughout this book, and it is an indication that you believe that Jesus is Lord, and you are blessed, for bless are the poor in spirit that is those who knows that they are spiritually bankrupt for theirs is the kingdom of heaven.

So Please Say This Prayer with me, but make sure you make It YOUR OWN so that it will come from your heart since you made the decision to respond to the call of SALVATION by opening the door of your heart to Him.

Let's Go, please

My Lord Jesus
Today l Come To You
Because l am a sinner and indeed of a Savior
I believe you are the son of God
I believe you died and rose from death
I make a decision today to receive you
As my Lord and my personal Savior
Please wash my sins in your precious blood
And write my name in the Book of Life
Thank you for the finished work on the cross
And thank you for saving a sinner like me
In Jesus' name l pray, AMEN.

Hallelujah!!! I will welcome you home in a minute but first, let me lead you to receive the spirit of God to make you completely lacking nothing.

The Holy Spirit Baptism

And it happened, while Apollos was at Corinth, that Paul, having passed through the upper regions, came to Ephesus. And finding some disciples he said to them, "Did you receive the Holy Spirit when you believed?" So, they said to him, "We have not so much as heard whether there is a Holy Spirit." And he said to them, "Into what then were you baptized?" So they said, "Into John's baptism." Then Paul said, "John indeed baptized with a baptism of repentance, saying to the people that they should believe on Him who would come after him, that is, on Christ Jesus." When they heard this, they were baptized in the name of the Lord Jesus. And when Paul had laid hands on them, the Holy Spirit came upon them, and they spoke with tongues and prophesied.

— ACT 19:1-6

I want you to receive the holy spirits by faith just as you receive Jesus Christ, please say this after me, Jesus I ask you to Baptist me in the Holy Spirit.

Now let me pray for you:

Jesus, I ask you to fill my brother or sister holding this book and has come to faith with your holy Spirit right now from the top of his or her head to the soul of their feet the same way the holy spirit came upon the disciples in the upper room and filled them and all those who came to faith, my Lord anoint him or her with the power of the holy spirit in your name, and I take authority over every spirit of fear, rejection, sickness, lack, delay, poverty, bitterness, malice, envy, jealousy , lie, addiction, any bandage that has healed him or her, my Lord every tree you have not planted in their lives l uproot them in your name, fill him or her with the joy in the holy ghost, with love, with peace, with meekness, with forgiveness, let the fruit of the holy spirit be seen in them, thank you, Jesus, for baptising them in the name of the father the son and the Holy Spirit, AMEN.

Now l officially Welcome you home the beloved of the Lord, this is the best decision you have ever made in your whole life, l wish you could see how not only the angles are rejoicing but God Himself singing and dancing for your homecoming because you were lost but now you are FOUND even though wide and broad is the gate that leads to distraction as the enemy is trapping mankind to enter thinking they will find rest for its seems that way, but you have figured out that that big gate is not were freedom is and have chosen the small and narrow gate for that is the road that leads to LIFE, we rejoice with Heavenly host hallelujahs to the king of kings who was slain for us and wounded for our transgressions, bruised for our iniquities; we thank this God who has taken the chastisement of our peace upon himself.

Look for a church to join in, it is especially important.

YOUR RELATIONSHIP WITH HIM

"When an unclean spirit goes out of a man, he goes through dry places, seeking rest, and finds none. Then he says, 'I will return to my house from which I came.' And when he comes, he finds it empty, swept, and put in order. Then he goes and takes with him seven other spirits more wicked than himself, and they enter and dwell there; and the last state of that man is worse than the first. So shall it also be with this wicked generation."

— MATTHEW 12:43-45

Okay, now that you are home, let me show you around a little bit and your Paster will do the rest by holding your hand and leading you through your daily walk with the Lord your God, as we are all work in progress in this Christ-like journey we have embarked on.

When we get delivered from the hands of our adversary remember old things have passed away everything has become new we can live, but to the enemy it's not over even though we are not his anymore, he will still try to come back and interestingly he called a person he was cast out from body his house, saying to himself 'I will return to my house which I came from as if he went out of the person by his choice or by his own doing, but because he is not low abiding, true to his word he will come and when he comes and finds it empty, swept and put in order which it will be because we have been set free but it will be EMPTY only if we are not filling it up with the Word of God, which will curse him to want to stay, and he thinks he was able to cast out because he was alone, so he goes and takes with him seven other spirits more wicked than himself, and they enter and dwell there, which makes the last state of that person worse than the first, but funny enough all of them can still be cast out in the same name Jesus, so l do not know if they think they can protect themselves if they are many and put their powers together or what but that is a discussion for the nest topic, but this time, what l want for you Is the importance of spending time with the Word of God.

A Draw near to God and He will draw near to you.

— JAMES 4:8

Christ is a person and just like any relationship if there is no time involved it is not going to work, when it Comes to you and your savor The kind of relationship you should have with Him should be even more solid than the relationship you have with men, because men can deceive you even when they are smiling with all their teeth out with you, we don't always get what we see from men but what you see from your God is actually what you get. Draw near to Him and you will see Him closer daily to you, for God is not only what is written but He is an experience, you can have an experience with Him, among our children the one closer to us is the one that gets the best out of us, it's the same with God, our walk with Him is a work in process and our mission is to be like Him one day for as He is so are we in this world.

"God is not a man, that He should lie, Nor a son of man, that He should repent. Has He said, and will He not do? Or has He spoken, and will He not make it good?

— NUMBERS 23:19

That is why He alone is trustworthy to have every conversation with and at the end of the day He is the only one who can help you anyway, men help is limited even if they have good intentions to help but Gods help is unlimited, and He is not a man who will lie to you, Moses posts this question to the children of Israel, has God spoken and did not do it? and the answer is NO He always comes through.

So the Lord gave to Israel all the land of which He had sworn to give to their fathers, and they took possession of it and dwelt in it. The Lord gave them rest all around, according to all that He had sworn to their fathers. And not a man of all their enemies stood against them; the Lord delivered all their enemies into their hands. Not a word failed of any good thing which the Lord had spoken to the house of Israel. All happened.

— JOSHUA 21: 43-45

That is how trustworthy He Is, He is your father tell Him your weakness, your strangles, things you don't understand ask the

Holy Spirit to help you remember you are not an orphan we are the children of the living God, When my mum went to be with the Lord, I said to her body you brought me here to this world and you left me here so if it wasn't for God who lives forever what would you expect me to do, so you are in good hands not in the hands of men who promise you today but leaves tomorrow, He will glorify Himself to you and May He alone be your best friend.

Delight yourself also in the Lord, And He shall give you the desires of your heart.

— PSALMS 37:4

Delight yourself also in the Lord, you see how important Christ is to you as I said at the end of the day He is our only help He is the only one who can give you your heart desires, study the Word daily and meditate on what He tells you through the Word and put your total trust in Him through His Word for He is the only TRUTH Look unto Him alone as He is your beginning and the end of your faith, He alone is your hero and your role model.

I have not departed from the commandment of His lips; I have treasured the words of His mouth More than my necessary food.

— JOB 23:12

Thy words were found, and I did eat them; and thy word was unto me the joy and rejoicing of mine heart: for I am called by thy name, O LORD God of hosts.

— JEREMIAH 15:16

The whole bible or the Word of God in totality can be defined as LOGOS, and every promise in there is for you and for your household, which can be also defined as RHEMA, so what Jeremiah is saying is he found RHEMA in the World and of God and eat them because they are true, yes and Amen which makes it rejoicing of his heart: Job will say he did not depart from the commandment of Gods lips; he treasured the Words of Gods mouth More than his necessary food. We Find the Word of God by spending time with it, that is how you eat it, since it's the only nourishment to our soul just as we cannot survive without physical food in our body, we cannot also survive without our spiritual FOOD called the Word of God being consumed.

This is what the demon who is trying to come back was talking about image you not eating physically, what strength will you have to fight anything or anyone? it's the same way spiritually, for you to resist the enemy you would first have to BELIEVE in God since that is where those who do exploits are found, for without Faith it will be impossible to please God, and it all starts with you seeing the importance of the Word to your soul it's our only Joy in this world, since we have become children of God, He has called us, so we are in this world even though we are not of this world because of our new status which is Gods adopted men and women. Let His truthful Word mean everything to you for they are LIFE to your soul and Medicine to your Borns, speak to Him about everything, what upsets you, what you do not understand for He is a friend indeed, draw near to Him and He will draw near to you.

THE ENEMY LS NOT LAW ABIDING

The thief does not come except to steal, to kill, and to destroy. I have come that they may have life, and that they may have it more abundantly.

— JOHN 10:10

Just as Some people will do whatever because of who they are, and even though there is a law that prohibits those actions, they are very much aware that if they get caught the law will deal with them, but it does not deter them from disobeying the law. That is who our adversary is, even though You have been purchased, delivered, washed by the blood of Jesus, and set free because of the transaction that took place which is the finished work of the cross, you would think that would deter the enemy since we have been redeemed but he does not understand that language, and since a thief does not come except to steal, to kill, and to destroy, God is saying to you, remember that He has also come that you may have life, and that you may have it more abundantly and He has overcome this world on your behalf.

Be sober, be vigilant; because your adversary the devil walks about like a roaring lion, seeking whom he may devour.

—1 PETER 5:8

The enemy walks about seeking his victims, and the reason why he has to SEEK his victims is that, he knows most of the redeemed of the Lord do not even know who they have become because of Jesus' death and His resurrection, so the enemy is standing on their ignorance to take advantage of them by selling them his many lies, of how Gods promises are not Yes and Amen in their lowest moments, so that he will get them to feel hopelessness, anxiousness, feeling forsaken and abandonment , basically all he is saying is, you cannot trust God in that situation and that circumstances, but meanwhile he knows the truth that at the mention of Jesus name every knee bow and every tongue confess that Jesus is LORD but because he is a deceiver his only purpose and plans is to deceive us. But what you should know is, just as you look in the marrow and do not forget how you looked when you step outside, please do not forget who the WORD of God says you are looking into the mirror of the living Word of God, because whoever He says you are is the TRUTH not what the situation is saying nor what the enemy is saying, everything shall pass away only the TRUTH abides. Our Lord says we are the head and not the tail, He says we are above and never beneath, and once has He spoken but twice have, we heard that all power belongs to Him because after He spoke, we are also repeating it every day that yes indeed all power belongs to our God and that settled it for us no matter what for what our Lord cannot do does not exist.

And why you should be bold in your faith in Christ is that you have been made to stand on this solid rock of ages Christ Jesus and His righteousness which is the unshakable kingdom and you know who you are period, Let say the enemy is afraid of dogs and l am a dog, and when the enemy came through whatever issues to try and see if l know who lam by testing the firm foundation am standing on, and he hears me crying like a cat, it means l do not know who lam and there is identity crisis going on with me, this is what is going on with many of us, and so please remember who God says you are being vigilant.

My people are destroyed for lack of knowledge.

— HOSEA 4:6A

Because you have rejected knowledge.

Our lack of knowledge of Him who has called us into glory and who He has turned us to be all because of the finished work of the cross has caused His own people to perish, it takes deliberate action to get to know who God has made you and the inheritance he has for the calling of His saints which is what you are now part of, for it is the truth we know that sets us free, after receiving Christ many settled just as children of God without any growth, but growing through the nourishment from the food you eat which is His Word and prayer is where maturity or sons and daughters can be found, those whom the enemy gets defeated by are those who know that He who is on their side is God Himself and His name will be exalted among the nations for them to know that The Lord of hosts is with us. The God of Jacob is your refuge. Selah, anytime you see this word SELAH it means stop or purse and reflect on what you just read, so am repeating that The God of Jacob is your refuge, so 1 want you to get to know Him for yourself, being just a child of God has coursed many of us to fall on the battlefield as we are fighting for our lives, our joy in the Lord, the good fare of our family, our peace, our marriages, our well-being, our finance and so on since life is heavy and complex for one to handle alone, salvation is just the beginning, and the knowledge most of us don't have is, we the redeemed of the Lord do not fight FOR victory we rather fight FROM the victory our Lord Jesus Christ which has been handed over to us, that is what makes the righteous as bold as a lion, that no matter what, God promises for us are Yes and Amen for victory belongs to the Lord our God.

For unto us a Child is born, unto us a Son is given; And the government will be upon His shoulder. And His name will be called Wonderful, Counsellor, Mighty God, Everlasting Father, Prince of Peace.

— ISAIAH 9:6

Unto us a (Child is born) but because a child cannot do anything, God waited for His growth in wisdom, His growth in knowledge, His growth in understanding where the government can be laid upon His shoulder, where He can perform His duties as Counsellor, taking the place of a Father, and being the Prince of Peace before Jesus was given unto us as a Son, we need to get to a place where no one can tell us anything contrary to what we know about Him Who is for us and not against us.

Now I say that the heir, as long as he is a child, does not differ at all from a slave, though he is master of all, but is under guardians and stewards until the time appointed by the father. Even so we, when we were children, were in bondage under the elements of the world. But when the fullness of the time had come, God sent forth His Son, born of a woman, born under the law, to redeem those who were under the law, that we might receive the adoption as sons.

— GALATIANS 4:1-5

Now I say that the heir, as long as he or she is a child, does not differ at all from a slave, even though he is master of all, this is what many children of God have become not knowing who they have become even though Christ has made us master of all, we get to know who we are and the intent of God for us through the word we here, and our personal relationship with Him, children are in bondage under the elements of the world because every wind can have their way in their life but when the fullness of the time comes because of the KNOWL-EDGE we have concerning the reason why Christ called us, we become unbreakable. What is the difference between a king and his whole army who were hiding from one man called Goliath and one person called David who took him out, the difference was clear, Goliath was calling them servants of the soul, but when David came he said we are not servant of soul we are the army of the most high God and defeated him, so it all came down to the knowledge David had about your God, in this life what you know and who you know is what holds us. As a lion roars, and goes over to its prey, a multitude of shep-herds can be summoned against the lion, but it will not be afraid of their voice, nor be disturbed by their noise, so is the

Lord of hosts who fights for Mount Zion and for its hill, which is you and your heart desires. He will be exalted on the earth! because of you.

YOU ARE A STRANGER LN THIS EARTH

Finally, my brethren, be strong in the Lord and in the power of His might. Put on the whole armor of God, that you may be able to stand against the wiles of the devil. For we do not wrestle against flesh and blood, but against principalities, against powers, against the rulers of the darkness of this age, against spiritual hosts of wickedness in the heavenly places. Therefore take up the whole armor of God, that you may be able to withstand in the evil day, and having done all, to stand. Stand therefore, having girded your waist with truth, having put on the breastplate of righteousness, and having shod your feet with the preparation of the gospel of peace; above all, taking the shield of faith with which you will be able to quench all the fiery darts of the wicked one. And take the helmet of salvation, and the sword of the Spirit, which is the word of God.

— EPHESIANS 6:10-17

Now that your spiritual understanding has been enlightened because you decided to be a partaker of God's kingdom, we have been told by our Lord God who created this world through His Word that, the way we used to see things and do things which is the natural way was wrong in the first place but that was all we were left with for being disobedience, but know that we have been turned into spirit back to our original state thanks to God whose mercies never ends, we have become strangers here on this planet, so we have to do things and see things in the way our Lord God sees them, for everything we see here is a result of what we do not see, which means LIFE is spiritual that is why we don't have much answers to the many questions we have as mankind, so how are we supposed to live now as children of God.

A Thus says the Lord: "Stand in the ways and see,

And ask for the old paths, where the good way is, And Walk in it.

Then you will find rest for your souls.

— JEREMAIAH 6:16

Throughout the scripture we have found out that those who come before us follow the manual of the manufacturer of this world which was given to them and that is what they left for us to follow which is the Word of God, is the manual written for our learning as the psalmist will say:

Open my eyes, that I may see Wondrous Things from Your law. I am a stranger in the earth; Do not hide Your commandments from me.

— PSALMS 119:18 -19

Thankfully our Lord God has never hidden His law or how He wants us to live from us and through Apostle Paul which is our first scripture Ephesians 6:10 -17, Apostle Paul is saying to you and everyone who has come to the faith that this is the way to go as a child of God, you should be strong in the Lord God whom you have placed your faith and hope in and in the power of His might, because we have no might nor power of our own to handle this life and all the complex things that come with it, and God by His grace and His mercies has provided us with Armory to for us to Put them on that we may be able to stand against the WILES of the devil, and you might be asking What are the WILES of the devil and what are the ARMOR of God.

First, the WILE of the devil is the trick or the stratagem he used intended to ensnare or to deceive us into thinking that Life is still flesh and blood and so we should treat things as such, everything that happens is physical, where there is no remedy for us since he has been winning for tricking us into thinking that the battle with him is natural because then all we could do is scratch the suffix but never to get to the truth of the matter, but to think of it he Satan and his acolytes who have made themselves our adversely, they are spirits, but they want us to fight or see life as flesh and blood even though we have been restated as spirits which is the original plan of God for us through the finished work of the cross, and what weapons are we going to even use to fight spiritual beings, but we are no more ignorance of their devices.

Now I, Paul, myself am pleading with you by the meekness and gentleness of Christ—who in presence am lowly among you, but being absent am bold toward you. But I beg you that when I am present I may not be bold with that confidence by which I intend to be bold against some, who think of us as if we walked according to the flesh. For though we walk in the flesh, we do not war according to the flesh. For the weapons of our warfare are not carnal but mighty in God for pulling down strongholds, casting down arguments and every high thing that exalts itself against the knowledge of God, bringing every thought into captivity to the obedience of Christ, and being ready to punish all disobedience when your obedience is fulfilled.

— CORINTHIANS 10, 2-6

That is why Paul is asking us to put on the spiritual Armory called the ARMOR OF GOD, which has been provided to us and will utterly destroy the enemy, REMEMBER our God who created us, and the enemy is a Spirit and made our enemy a spirit only, and even though we were created as spiritual beings also we were given flesh to house us, so we are not the flesh and blood as we see, our true nature is SPIRIT just as our father in Heaven, your main personality is your spirit that live inside your body. The enemy managed to kill us spiritually through our parents Adam and Eve so that we would be left with our house which is our physical being only so that he will have dominion over us for the flesh profit nothing it's the spirit that gives life, but GLORY BE TO GOD ALMIGHTY whom through our Lord Jesus Christ have restored us back spiritually to our rightful place having right standing with Him again become of the finished work on the cross.

So, the truth is, everything that happens to mankind has nothing to do with the physical, it all originated from the spiritual realm before it was seen physically it was originated from the spiritual realm, the world does not have the light who is Jesus Christ because Satan has managed to keep them in the dark, lest they received the light of Christ and began to see that we are not wrestling against flesh and blood or anything we see, but against principalities, against powers, against the rulers of the darkness of this age, against spiritual hosts of wickedness in the heavenly places.

Therefore, you should take up the whole armor of God, that you may be able to withstand in the evil day, the ARMOR of God is, first, we should stand therefore, having girded our waist with truth, and what is the TRUTH, the Truth is Jesus Christ; therefore, it makes every Word spoken by Him in what we called the bible True. so, we gird our waist with the TRUTH no matter what anybody says contrary to what God has said.

We have the TRUTH on our side, so you should CAST DOWN every thought, imagination, argument, and every high thing that exalts itself against the knowledge of God's Word, bringing every thought into captivity to the obedience of Christ.

The nest ARMOR is the BREASTPLATE of RIGHT-EOUSNESS' God made you righteous in Christ, you did nothing to earn it, it's a gift so do not let our accuser the devil who will make you feel like because of your short forth you cannot go before God or you are not worthy of Gods blessings, we are work in progress to perfection and God want us to come before Him boldly, for even if anything He is the only one who can fix us since He made us, so do not emit anything, because that is what those who fells unrighteous do, that is why you boldly display your BREASTPLATE of righteousness since it's a Gift.

The nest Armor is to shod our FEET with the preparation of the gospel of peace by telling others about the good news concerning the free gift you have received for them to receive it also, for we are save to serve just as am telling you about Jesus Christ and if you cannot wittiness to them just buy them this books for them to also come to the faith emptying heal and feeling up heaven, and take the SHIELD OF FAITH that is your faith in Jesus, with which you will be able to quench all the fiery darts of the wicked one. This is referring to Satan's temptation's that are like fiery arrows, you extinguished them with the shield of faith. you should really hold on to your FAITH in Christ for the enemy will do everything to for it through situations and circumstances in our lower moments is when he brings about his lies that God does not care or He will not help and all his devises that he uses to ensnare us, but Stand tall in your faith and you will the true lie if its God who has promise and not fail or its the already defeated enemy who has no truth in him.

And take the HELMET OF YOUR SALVATION, Jesus has become your SALVATION He is your song and your strength, He died and gave you that crown He is the author of our salvation and THE SWORD OF THE SPIRIT which is the Word of God to stand firm in your journey with Christ, when it comes to the Word of God, as I said before studding only what is writing without having a relationship with the Holy Spirit who is be hide the letter which is the scripture is just ten percent job than, as most do, they can court scriptures but what they don't know is what makes the scripture works is because of the Holy Spirit. Before Gods creation, we have been told that the earth was without form, void, and total darkness was on the face of the deep, and it's the Spirit of God who hover over it for God to do His thing, after God created us with dust for us to become living beings it was the Spirit of God that was bread into us, it was the Spirit of God who come to dwell in Mery, it was Him who resurrected Christ, He was the helper Jesus left us with, as you can see that your relationship with Him is the key, there is a difference between knowing about someone based on what people says and knowing them personally, the fact that we know what to take when we had a headache doe does not mean we are doctors there is still difference, knowing everything about Him through the scripture and also through your relationship with Him is how you become wonder to many, if you say you know someone it means you have a relationship with that person.

Faith comes by hearing, the beginning of sin which led to our downfall in the first place stated with a conversation that happened between our mother Eve and Satan which she and our father Adam acted upon, so you must only pay attention to what edify your soul.

> O Lord, I know the way of man is not in himself; It is not in man who walks to direct his own steps.
>
> — JEREMIAH 10:23

Our ways are not even in ourselves, that is how blind we are as mortal Men, our ways may seem good but at the end of it, its death, God may Redirect your steps to do things you may not always understand but He is the one who established your steps and He may lead you around, but He will not lead you wrong.

I am the door. If anyone enters by Me, he will be saved, and will go in and out and find pasture.

— JOHN 10:9

You will find pasture in Him for you and your loved ones, for you have been entered by Him who is the true joy, peace, and hope the entire world is seeking for.

HOW DO L EXPLAIN THE LOVE OF GOD TOWARDS YOU

How precious is Your lovingkindness, O God! Therefore the children of men put their trust under the
shadow of Your wings. They are abundantly satisfied
with the fullness of Your house, And You give them
drink from the river of Your pleasures. For with You is
the fountain of life; In Your light we see light.

— PSALMS 36:7-9

To explain the Gods love for you is like me being ask to drain
the sea dry which is an impossible takes for mankind, so what
shall l say or how do l describe it then, well, all l can say to you
is to repeat what the psalmists is saying here to your Lord God,
that His lovingkindness is the reason why the children of men
especially you, have putting their trust under the shadow of
His wings, just as you have done today for the safest place to
hide in this land of the living is in the name of our Lord Jesus
Christ, He is our only strong and fortified tower a very present
help in times of trouble so the righteous run into Him and we

are safe, you have become part of the righteousness of God for we the redeemed of the Lord have been made righteous, it's a gift from God to all who have received Christ as their Lord and personal savior, so do not take yourself out anytime you here righteous people, we are now righteous because of what Christ has done not because we did anything to deserve it. We are abundantly satisfied with the fullness of His house just as you will be, for He gives us drink from the river of His pleasures, with Him is the fountain of life; with all the dankness that has covered the earth we can see because of His light.

> Who is he who condemns? It is Christ who died, and furthermore is also risen, who is even at the right hand of God, who also makes intercession for us.
>
> — ROMANS 8:34

With our relationship with men you know how it goes the good we do mostly get buried with our bones, but the evil we do seems not to be overlooked, meanwhile its only our Lord who can condemn us since He is the only righteous and the only one who died for us, and furthermore, also risen and amazingly in-stand of Him condemning you and us He is rather sitting at the right of God, making intercession for us. So now the question is, who shall then separate you from the love of Christ? there's none as you can see, it doesn't matter who accuse you of what is not from your Lord, our righteousness is a gift from God, the one who gave it to you is on your side.

> The Lord has appeared of old to me, saying: "Yes, I have loved you with an everlasting love; Therefore, with lovingkindness I have drawn you.

— JEREMIAH 31:3

His love for you and us, is of old which has no end as He calls it, Himself, the everlasting love; Therefore, with lovingkindness He has drawn you, He will be there with you and for you just know that He care so may you never question His Love for you when it gets to a point where you don't see His Hands meaning your answers, the enemy may try to make you feel as though Gods promises are not YES and AMEN, but remember his schemes that he has no truth in him, so just trust the HEART of your Lord God as His hands shall follow too, because of His trustworthiness.

YOU WHO FOLLOW AFTER (RIGHTEOUSNESS)

"Listen to Me, you who follow after righteousness, You who seek the Lord: Look to the rock from which you were hewn, and to the hole of the pit from which you were dug. Look to Abraham your father, and to Sarah who bore you; For I called him alone, And blessed him and increased him." For the Lord will comfort Zion, He will comfort all her waste places; He will make her wilderness like Eden, And her desert like the garden of the Lord; Joy and gladness will be found in it, Thanksgiving and the voice of melody.

— ISAIAH 51:1-3

Christ is saying, as you have decided to follow after Him, do not forget to remember or to Look to the ROCK from which you were hewn, and to the hole of the PIT from which you were dug, meaning, our father and Mother Abraham and Sarah were nothing but some downcast people but look at what He turn them into when He called them and be comforted as you are also seeking after RIGHTEOUSNESS who is Jesus. He called them alone blessed and increased them,." the Lord you have placed your hope and trust in want you to know that He can change any situation at all, take it from how He turned things around for Abraham and Sarah, He gives His beauty to the one who is covered in ashes, He raises the poor from the dust and lifts the beggar from the ash heap just to set them among princes and make them inherit the throne of glory. He is able to do anything "For the pillars of the earth are His, and He has set the world upon them. He has called you to the same blessing for those blessing He gave Abraham were not just for them but for all the seed of Abraham which is everyone who has come to the faith which you are a partaker of the righteousness of God in Christ Jesus and that makes you the heir of His inheritance, so the blessings of Abraham are yours.

The Lord said He will comfort Zion, the Zion represents you, He will comfort all your waste places; He will make your wilderness like Eden, and her desert like the garden of the Lord, if the Lord your God has made your wilderness and your desert which represent whatever issues you are facing His garden comforting your waste places; why wouldn't the one who is your Joy and gladness be found in your Thanksgiving through the voice of your melody.

For thus says the Lord, Who created the heavens, Who is God, Who formed the earth and made it, Who has established it, Who did not create it in vain, Who formed it to be inhabited: l am the Lord and there is no other. l have not spoken in secret In a dark place of the earth; l did not say to the seed of Jacob, Seek me in vain'; l the Lord, Speak righteousness, l declare things that are right.

— ISAIAH 45:18-19

The Lord said because He knows who He is and what He is capable of, that's why He has not promised you in secret. His promises to you are open as He tells you to seek Him because He will back His promised up with DEEDS, for what He cannot do does not exist, the Lord your God who created heaven and earth is the one watering your life that means Joy, gladness, thanksgiving and the voice of melody has no option but to be found in your mouth , He will see you through it all in every step of the way, He will do whatever He says He will do, am telling you the truth it does not matter how loud the enemy and the situation are screaming Trust in your Lord God and the power of His might for He is Almighty indeed.

HOW THE PROMISE WILL HAPPEN
IS HIS DOING

"But you, Bethlehem Ephrathah, Though you are little among the thousands of Judah, Yet out of you shall come forth to Me The One to be Ruler in Israel, Whose goings forth are from of old, From everlasting."

— MICAH 5:2

God gave a promise through prophet Micah concerning the city where the birth of our Lord Jesus Christ will take place and that's Bethlehem but that city was not where those chosen to bring about the promise were dwelling, Joseph and Mary lived in Galilee out of the city of Nazareth so it seems like that is where the baby was going to be born since they were there throughout the full term of the pregnancy but SOMETHING HAPPENED.

And it came to pass in those days that a decree went out from Caesar Augustus that all the world should be registered. This census first took place while Quirinius was governing Syria. So all went to be registered, everyone to his own city. Joseph also went up from Galilee, out of the city of Nazareth, into Judea, to the city of David, which is called Bethlehem, because he was of the house and lineage of David.

— LUKE 2:1-4

The king at that time called Caesar Augustus decided he was going to continue taxation on the people, they made the journey to where Joseph was born to be registered, as everyone went to be registered, everyone to his own city, and it happens that it was time for baby Jesus to be born which even the parents didn't know it was going to be that day, I hope you can see the hand of God working His wonders through this king, this is what took Joseph from Galilee, out of the city of Nazareth, to Judea, to the city of David, which is called Bethlehem, because he was of the house and lineage of David, immediately they got there Mary had the baby, you see how God brought to pass His promise if that was said to Joseph and Mary directly that the baby will be born in Bethlehem I believe they would be asking themselves question as the pregnancy got to it full term, but He has promise and He will never fail.

The Lord gave them rest all around, according to all that He had sworn to their fathers. And not a man of all their enemies stood against them; the Lord delivered all their enemies into their hands.

Not a word failed of any good thing which the Lord had spoken to the house of Israel. All happened.

— JOSHUA 21:44-45

He has lifted His Word above Himself that's how important His Word is to Him, His faithfulness is forever and even more, what He has said concerning your life take it to the bank because it can be cashed. Trust Him on His Word even if you do not understand His ways of doing things, all of us do not understand Him because His ways of doing things are not the same as men, so just trust His heart and obey for His thoughts towards you are thoughts of peace and not evil like men, as I always say if men say to you, look up, you better look down, but not this God of yours, Joseph brothers thought they are stopping him from becoming somebody important than them because of the kind of dreams he was having not knowing where they sold him to be is the actual country he was going to be somebody important, the enemy thought killing Jesus was the way to stop Him from saving all of us but little did they know that just as a farmer will plant a corn in the grounds but rip abundance that was act actually was they were doing, and know see what has happened.

O Lord, I know the way of man is not in himself.

It is not in man who walks to direct his own steps.

— JEREMAIAH 10:23

This is what prophet Jeremiah said to your Lord, you can see from this small example I have given you that anyone or even Satan Himself who will fight you does not even know what they are doing as your Lord God will prove to them that He created everyone and everything and His understanding is beyond us for its unsearchable, this is why I want you to hold on tight to Him, your Lord Jesus Christ is all you need in this land of the living till He takes us home.

VICTORY HAS A VOICE

So when this corruptible has put on incorruption, and this mortal has put on immortality, then shall be brought to pass the saying that is written: "Death is swallowed up in victory."

— 1 CORINTHIANS 15:54

Death could only be swallowed up if victory has a mouth, The Lord is saying there were times in our lives we did have on corruptible nature because of the fall of men, and so we were not in the position to declare anything because of our sinful nature, we were cursed because of our sin, and what does one expects from someone who is coursed, we did not have any option but leave according to our kind for a tree can only produce its kind, and we were known by our fruit and the kind of tree we were, but after receiving the gift Christ gave us through the shed of His blood, we become new creature just as you have become today, and now had on in-corruption which is the true nature of God so now we can declare things like our daddy and do all things true Christ who strengthens us and bring to pass the saying that is written: "Death is [swallowed up in victory."] we can now boldly declare by telling any mountain that presents itself to us that you have been swallowed in victory since we have been delivered from the course of the law, we have been given the platform which is the victory of Christ on our behalf to declare a thing and it shall be established. DEATH and LIFE has been placed on our thong and whatever we chose to do with it, we will eat the fruits of it, what l want to tell you is this, as someone who has the nature of God you can proclaim the things you want to see tomorrow, not the situation you are in, but the position we want to find yourself in tomorrow, that's why the WEEK says they are strong in their weaknesses, the poor says they are rich in their lack, the barring women can say she has seven children in their barrenness, the sick can confidently say they are healed not because we have lost our mind but because our father who has adopted us into His kingdom is a SPIRIT and that's the way He goes about and does His things, and we are on the His side not on the side of the world and the way they do things anymore, the world we once belong to says don't say you are healed if the evident is saying you are sick, the barring woman cannot sing for there is nothing to rejoice for, the week cannot say they are strong for the evidence is saying they are week, the poor cannot not say they are rich according to World were we came from people who believe in what God has said have lost their mind as we all know since we use to be part of that thoughts.

Now you are the body of Christ, and members individually.

—1 CORINTHIANS 12:27

Jesus said I only do the things I has seen my father do, that is
what we, His children whom He has turned into spirit also do
and says the things we have seen our Lord Jesus has asked us to
do and says, we have been told by our Lord to have faith in
Him for with Him all things are possible, so we declare in faith
the promises of God for you on yourself, on your children, on
your family on the works of your hands on your body for
victory has a voice God created this world with His WORD,
it's our soul that is saved and not our body or our flesh, this
body of ours is still on the world's side, and would want its old
way to rule, that is, if you say you are healed it has to be
because it is visible to the five senses that you are truly healed,
which is SEE, TEST, TOUCH, HERE, and FEEL, just as the
world sees them, other than that, it may look like you are lying,
and those around you who do not understand the way your
God operates will say the same that you have lost your mind,
but we know the truth that God who created us in His own
image spoke and they came to pass for nothing we see physically will be here if it wasn't for the spiritual realm or the
things we don't see, Everything we see CAME from the unseen
or spiritual world that's how we operate like father like sons
and daughters. so don't expect people to understand you or
speak your language

It is the Spirit who gives life; the flesh profits nothing.
The words that I speak to you are spirit, and they are
life.

— JOHN 6:63

The one who has adopted you is a Spirit and He is saying to
you no matter what your five senses and those who belong to
this world and even some of those who have come to Christ

and lack faith may say, because they will, always remember that It is the Spirit who gives life; for the flesh profit nothing and so the Words that He has spoken to you are Spirit, and they are life, the flesh that is telling you to see 10 billion dollars in your account before you are allowed to say that you have that amount of money profits nothing because it does not have the truth, the truth is what your spirit says, the week says he or she is strong, even though he or she may be week physically, but we are not moved by what we see, we are only moved by the Word of God, know and understand that we are beneficiaries of what Christ has done for us on the cross, who can deny something that has already happened.

He has already gone through the crucifixions, so all things are ours, that is why we are declaring what we want to see happen tomorrow, the world declares what they are going through, but we the redeem of the Lord declare what we want to see, that is the difference between us and them is not that you or the rest of us have lost our mind by saying we are healed whiles the facts are showing otherwise, we are just on the Lord's side, and we have been told to call those things we want that be not as though they were.

The heavens declare the glory of God; And the firmament shows His handiwork.

Day unto day utters speech, And night unto night reveals knowledge.

— PSALMS 19:1-2

Everything speaks in this world even the heavens declare the glory of God, Day unto day utters speech, and night unto night reveals knowledge, Day utters speech to Day and night reveals knowledge tonight, this is the mystery the world does not know but it has been revealed to us, the light of Christ has shone on the truth that was hiding from us because of where we use to be, so is not that we are crazy it's because we know something the world does not know, they will cash up later only if they come to the light who is the lamp unto our feet directing our every step and the light unto our path given us a clear picture of what our future with Him looks like, very colourful and bright. The Word of God asks us to do something, which is, He wants His redeemed to SAY so, you have been redeemed so proclaim redemption from every lack, delay, sickness, anxiety and so on every day, this is the Perfect Revelation of the Lord.

> And in that day, you will say: "Praise the Lord, call upon His name; Declare His deeds among the peoples, Make mention that His name is exalted.

> — ISAIAH 12:4

This is my prayer for you because of what your Lord God has stated to do and will continue to do for you and the lives of your love once , it will course you to Praise the Lord, and call upon His name always by declaring His deeds among the people around you, as you will make mention of Him to others that Christ name is exalted, for you are in God's hands, not in the hands of men who cannot be trusted but the hands of your Lord God Almighty who is a hiding place for us.

YOU WILL INHERIT IT THROUGH PATIENCE AND COMFORT

For whatever things were written before were written for our learning, that we through the patience and comfort of the Scriptures might have hope.

— ROMANS 15:4

Hope in the Lord your God is the only tool you have so you cannot afford to lose hope no matter what, as Satan through life and its issues will challenge you remember Christ has overcome this world and He is your anchor to help you navigate through this life, remember again that we are not fighting FOR victory we are rather fighting FROM victory, because Christ has won it all already.

Every single Word written was written for our learning, so that we will also know what to do by holding on to these two PATIENCE and COMFORT knowing that He who has promised is faithful.

And we desire that each one of you show the same diligence to the full assurance of hope until the end, that
you do not become sluggish but imitate those who
through faith and patience inherit the promises.

— HEBREWS 6:11-12

Apostle Paul is saying, that what they desire for you and all of
us is that each one of us will show the same diligence to the
full assurance of hope until the end as long as there is life, just
as they also did the want us to imitate them, it got to a time in
the life of our father Abraham, he has to even hope against
hope but truly he received the promise, you are not hearing
something different or are they telling us something they
knew nothing about, as to how this world works, we are being
given the road map they used to get to the VICTORY place of
life, first and foremost you are already a winner for you are on
the winning side who is Christ our Lord.

A Stand therefore, having girded your waist with truth.

— EPHESIANS 6:14

What He says is what will stands forever because He is the
TRUTH and it's the truth we know that sets as free, everything
and every other words will pass away only the truth abides, so
you should stand your ground because we have an unshakeable
kingdom and it's not even everyone who is save that has faith
or might have faith like you, for there are many children of
God who does not have faith and because of that, many are
fallen on the battle field as the Lord God said Himself my
people perish for lack of knowledge, this journey is a personal
journey and so if your five senses and the world who are not

save by the blood of Jesus and even those saved but lacks faith are seeing things the same way as this world sees them, Stand therefore, having girded your waist with the TRUTH you know no matter what and see who will have the last laugh, Jesus said because my word is yes and Amen is why l did not spoke to you in the deck place when l say to you believe in me and seek me but l promise you openly, because l can back up my Word by doing what l say l will do.

For you have need of endurance, so that after you have done the will of God, you may receive the promise.

— HEBREW 10:36

Pertinence and endurance are needed for us to be able to get to where our Lord expects us to be, we are following the foot-steps of those before us and as they look to God and their faces are not ashamed, you who are looking to God your face will not be ashamed too for He is the same yesterday and today. He cannot deny Himself that He is good, and His mercies endured forever.

YOU ARE NOT BEATEN THE AIR

And everyone who competes for the prize is temperate in all things. Now they do it to obtain a perishable crown, but we for an imperishable crown.

Therefore I run thus: not with uncertainty. Thus I fight: not as one who beats the air.

— 1 CORINTHIANS 9:25-26

The world competes for a perishable crown and you know the lent they go through to get it, we are looking forward to an imperishable crown how then do you think we should go about it, that is why we run in faith in Him not with uncertainty nor like one who beats the air, but we discipline our body and bring it into subjection, casting down everything that exult itself against the knowledge of God because we have found the light who is the truth, so the truth is on our side.

"Sing, O barren, You who have not borne! Break forth into singing, and cry aloud, You who have not laboured with child! For more are the children of the desolate Than the children of the married woman," says the Lord.

"Enlarge the place of your tent, and let them stretch out the curtains of your dwellings; do not spare; Lengthen your cords, And strengthen your stakes. For you shall expand to the right and to the left, And your descendants will inherit the nations, and make the desolate cities inhabited.

"Do not fear, for you will not be ashamed; neither be disgraced, for you will not be put to shame; for you will forget the shame of your youth, and will not remember the reproach of your widowhood anymore.

For your Maker is your husband, the Lord of hosts is His name; and your Redeemer is the Holy One of Israel; He is called the God of the whole earth.

— ISAIAH 54:1-5

You can sing and rejoice over the things that are not yet visible to the naked eye for your Lord God has done it all for you is just a matter of time. Because of what He has done, He is boldly saying to you do not fear, for you will not be ashamed neither will you be disgraced for believing in Him, one thing is for sure, and that is, you will forget the shame of your youth. You will not remember the reproach of your widowhood-which is the lost peace the lost joy the lost marriage everything your past brought your way that course your pain will not be remembered anymore, for your Maker who is the husband of His church has a name which is The Lord of hosts your Redeemer the Holy One of Israel; He is your sharped, the light unto your path, and the lifted up of your head, He has made a Perpetual Covenant of Peace with you to be your help.

STAY BLESS AND REMEMBER WHO IS ON THE THROWN

May the Lord God who has made a way for me to be in your home through this book course your way to shine with the brightness of His true light, May the obedience of Joseph, the joy of the Angels, the eagerness of the shepherds and the determination of the Might of God that brought forth this unimaginable blessing, manifest the same wonders in your life and the lives of your love once, as your days are so shall your strength be in the name of Jesus Christ our Saviour, l pray, Amen.

These unimaginable blessings.

Your servant the evangelist
Emmanuela S Lewis
Alias Miss Peggy

ACKNOWLEDGMENTS

Suppose by the grace of God I am in your hands and your homes through this book.

In that case, this book has found you well because the purpose of this book is to tell you about the only good news that will change your life forever, it will give your soul rest from its restlessness all because of the change that is bound to happen in the fundamental core of your very being and lift you up for you to grab your reservation ticket that places you beside our Lord who rings forever and ever.